W9-CLM-693

ENDANGERED ANIMALS

SEA OTTERS

BY PATRICIA HUTCHISON

Published by The Child's World®
1980 Lookout Drive • Mankato, MN 56003-1705
800-599-READ • www.childsworld.com

Acknowledgments
The Child's World®: Mary Berendes, Publishing Director
Red Line Editorial: Editorial direction and production
The Design Lab: Design
Amnet: Production

Design Element: Shutterstock Images
Photographs ©: Shutterstock Images, cover, 1, 10; US
Fish and Wildlife Service, 4; Laura MK/iStockphoto, 6–7;
iStockphoto, 8, 20; Only Fabrizio/Shutterstock Images, 11,
22; Hulton-Deutsch Collection/Corbis, 12; Rob Stapleton/
AP Images, 14; Michael Yang/Rex Features/AP Images,
16; Ryan M. Bolton/Shutterstock Images, 18–19; Doug
Meek/Shutterstock Images, 21

ISBN 9781631439728
LCCN 2014959643

Printed in the United States of America
Mankato, MN
July, 2015
PA02264

ABOUT THE AUTHOR

A former teacher, Patricia Hutchison enjoys traveling with her family. She's seen sea otters swirl and swim off the coast of Big Sur, California. Hutchison enjoys writing books for children about science and nature.

TABLE OF CONTENTS

CHAPTER ONE

WET WEASELS

Sea otters spend most of their lives in the Pacific Ocean.

Sea otters swim in the cold ocean water. They dive down to the bottom. They pop up on the surface to breathe. Sea otters live in the Pacific Ocean. They are found along the coast from California to Alaska. They are also found along the coast of northeast Asia. These otters can live their whole lives without leaving the ocean.

Sea otters are **mammals**. They are the largest members of the weasel family. Ferrets and badgers are weasels, too. Sea otters are the smallest **marine** mammal. Sea otters' bodies are made for the water. They have slim bodies that grow to about 4 feet (1 m) long. They weigh from

Sea otters are built for swimming.

Body Parts of a Sea Otter

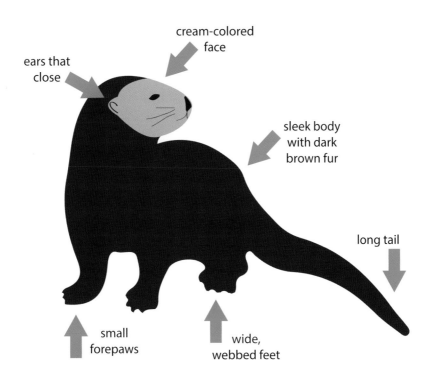

cream-colored face

ears that close

sleek body with dark brown fur

long tail

small forepaws

wide, webbed feet

45 to 65 pounds (20 to 29 kg). Their webbed feet help them swim. A sea otter can close its ears when it dives. It can close its nostrils, too. Flat tails help otters move around in the water.

The ocean water stays cold. Its temperature is between 35 and 60 degrees Fahrenheit (2 to 16° C). Otters do not use body fat to keep warm. Instead their fur is very **dense**. Each square inch of an otter has approximately 645,000 hairs. A person has

Two layers of fur keep sea otters warm.

Otters eat a lot of shellfish, including crabs.

about 100,000 hairs on his or her head. A sea otter's fur has two layers. The bottom layer is dark brown. The upper layer is light brown. Air gets trapped between the layers. The air helps keep otters warm.

Sea otters live in kelp forests. In the brown seaweed, otters find their food. They eat shellfish, small fish, and other creatures. Sea otters eat a lot. Otters can eat 20 clams in one hour. Sea otters also eat snails, mussels, and crabs. Unlike most marine mammals, sea otters can drink salt water. Their large **kidneys** filter the salt water. Then their bodies can use the freshwater.

The otters store food in loose skin under their armpits. They carry food up to the water's surface to eat. Sea otters use rocks to open shells. They put the rocks on their chests. They smash the shellfish against the rocks. Eventually the shells break. The otters take out their meals and slurp them down.

Sea otters usually give birth to one **pup** each year. Sometimes a mother may have twins. The baby pups are born in the water. Newborn pups are about 2 feet (0.6 m) long. They weigh from 4 to 5 pounds (1.8 to 2.3 kg). Each has a

LET'S EAT!

Swimming, diving, and keeping warm use up energy. Otters need to eat one-fourth of their weight each day to stay alive. How much is that? A 60-pound (27-kg) human child would need to eat 15 pounds (7 kg) of food a day. That is about 150 hot dogs!

thick coat of baby fur. The fur acts like a life jacket. Sea otter babies are **buoyant**. For the first few months, they cannot dive. Instead they float on the surface. Their mothers feed them for the first eight months of their lives. First they just drink their mothers' milk. After two months, they start looking for other food with their mothers' help.

Female sea otters and their pups often live together in a group. Males live in a different group. Both groups sleep in the kelp forests. Sea otters wrap themselves up in kelp to sleep.

Infant sea otters have thick, fuzzy coats.

The seaweed keeps them from floating away. Mothers wrap their babies in kelp, too. Then they dive for food. They know their babies will not float away.

Sea otters like to groom themselves often. Their loose skin can be easily pulled. An otter can pull on its skin to reach and clean all its fur. But grooming is a tough job. Otters twist in the water, turning somersaults. First they squeeze water out of their fur. Then they fluff it and blow air into it. This traps air bubbles against their skin. The air helps keep the otters warm.

Sea otters often strike funny poses when they groom themselves.

CHAPTER TWO

OTTERS AT RISK

The fur trade nearly caused the sea otter to become extinct.

Before the 1700s, 100,000 to 300,000 sea otters swam in
the Pacific Ocean. But people wanted their beautiful, warm
furs. Traders hunted them in the 1700s and 1800s. They killed

the otters and took their furs. They sold the furs, which were made into capes and belts. By the early 1900s, fewer than 2,000 sea otters were left.

Sea otters have other **predators**. Sharks and killer whales hunt them. Eagles and bears eat them, too. However, humans are bigger threats. Oil spills and **pollution** spoil otter **habitat**. People enjoy some of the same foods as sea otters. There is less food for the otters to eat. Human activities have caused sea otters to become **endangered**.

Oil spills are the biggest threat to sea otters. The oil tangles their fur. It sticks to their bodies. The fur cannot trap air inside its layers. The otters can die from the cold. Oil is also poisonous to sea otters. It damages their kidneys, lungs, and eyes. In 1989 the Exxon Valdez oil tanker had an accident in Alaska. Eleven million gallons (42 million L) of oil spilled into the ocean. The oil killed at least 2,800 sea otters. Scientists think a large oil spill in California could wipe out all the sea otters there.

The otter on the right has oil on its fur, while the otter on the left does not.

Pollution also threatens sea otters. Humans dump waste into the water. Some of it settles on the ocean floor. It harms the shellfish living there. The otters then eat the shellfish. This can make the otters very sick. Pollution is not the only threat to an otter's food. People like to eat shellfish, too.

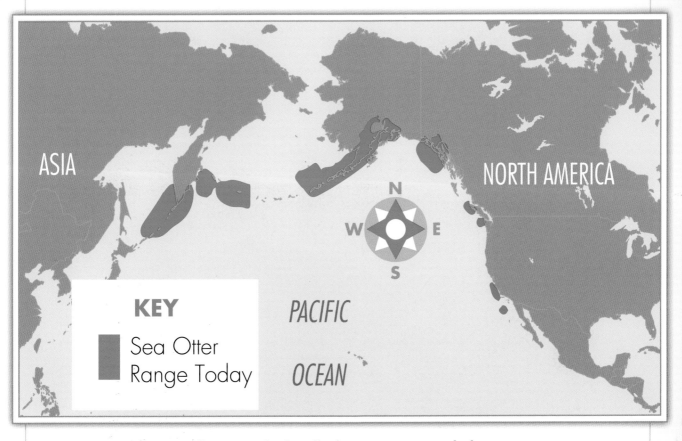

**Pollution and oil spills threaten sea otter habitat
in the northern Pacific Ocean.**

Sometimes sea otters fish in the same areas as humans. The
otters may be shot. Or they may become trapped in fishing
nets. Then they drown.

HELPING THE KELP

*Sea otters help keep kelp beds healthy. Shellfish eat kelp. Sea otters eat shellfish.
Without sea otters, the shellfish would take over. The kelp beds would die. When sea
otters are healthy, the kelp beds are healthy, too.*

HELPING SEA OTTERS

An otter swims in its exhibit at the Monterey Bay Aquarium.

By 1900 sea otters were almost **extinct**. In 1911 many countries signed a law. The law made it illegal to kill marine mammals for their fur. In 1972 the United States passed the Marine Mammal Protection Act. This act made it illegal to harm sea otters and other marine mammals. Humans cannot feed, hunt, capture, collect, or kill these animals. There are now approximately 106,000 sea otters in the world.

Some groups help sea otters. The Monterey Bay Aquarium in California has a sea otter program. People there rescue and treat injured otters. They also find pups that have lost their mothers. Female otters at the aquarium raise the pups. Many of the rescued otters are released. But sometimes that is not possible. Then the aquarium cares for them for the rest of their lives.

The aquarium also researches otters. Released otters have tags. Scientists use the tags to track and watch the otters. This helps scientists learn about the dangers otters face in the wild. Scientists also study dead sea otters. They look at the otters' blood to find out what killed them. The information helps scientists find ways to increase the number of wild otters.

The Otter Project also helps otters. This group watches over certain areas along the California coast. People come from all over to visit these areas. The Otter Project helps keep the water clean. Volunteers make sure people respect the animals and the environment.

Other groups restore and protect clean seawater. They help pass laws to reduce water pollution. They want to make sure the water is safe for

People come to California to watch sea otters.

Cleaning up ocean and beach pollution helps protect otter habitat.

drinking, swimming, and fishing. This helps sea otters live healthy lives in the wild.

Efforts of scientists and other groups have helped increase the number of wild sea otters. In 100 years, otter numbers increased from a few thousand to more than

100,000. But sea otters remain endangered. Humans must continue to work for the sea otters.

With help from humans, sea otters will continue to swim in the cold waters of the Pacific Ocean.

WHAT YOU CAN DO

- Be aware of what you put down the drain. Most of it will make its way into streams, rivers, and then into the ocean.

- Marine animals can get tangled up in plastic rings for drinks. This can hurt or drown the animals. Cut up the rings before you throw them away.

- Your classroom can adopt a sea otter from the Defenders of Wildlife through their Wildlife Adoption and Gift Center. The money goes to programs that help sea otters.

- Learn more about ocean pollution. Share what you learn with others.

GLOSSARY

buoyant (BOY-unt) Something that is buoyant is able to float. The air between a sea otter's layers of fur makes it buoyant.

dense (dens) A dense object has parts that crowd together. The fur of a sea otter is very dense.

endangered (en-DANE-jerd) An endangered animal is in danger of becoming extinct. Sea otters are endangered.

extinct (ek-STINKT) If a type of animal is extinct, all the animals have died out. If not protected, sea otters may become extinct.

habitat (HAB-i-tat) A habitat is a place where an animal lives. The Pacific Ocean is the sea otters' habitat.

kidneys (KID-neez) Kidneys are organs that remove waste from blood and make urine. Oil can damage a sea otter's kidneys.

mammals (MAM-alz) Mammals are animals that are warm-blooded, give birth to live young, and are usually covered with hair. Sea otters are mammals.

marine (muh-REEN) Marine means relating to the sea. Sea otters, seals, and whales are marine mammals.

pollution (puh-LOO-shun) Pollution is made up of substances that make land, water, and air unsafe. Ocean pollution spoils otter habitat.

predators (PRED-a-terz) Predators hunt, kill, and eat other animals. Sea otters have several predators in the wild.

pup (pup) A pup is a young otter. Otter mothers usually give birth to one pup each year.

TO LEARN MORE

BOOKS

Benoit, Peter. *The Exxon Valdez Oil Spill.* New York: Children's Press, 2011.

King, Zelda. *Sea Otters.* New York: PowerKids, 2012.

Marsh, Laura. *Sea Otters.* Washington, DC: National Geographic, 2014.

WEB SITES

Visit our Web site for links about sea otters:
childsworld.com/links

Note to Parents, Teachers, and Librarians: We routinely verify our Web links to make sure they are safe and active sites. So encourage your readers to check them out!

INDEX